HOW SHOULD THE
SOVEREIGNTY OF GOD
STRENGTHEN ME?

DAVID B. MCWILLIAMS

REFORMATION HERITAGE BOOKS
GRAND RAPIDS, MICHIGAN

How Should the Sovereignty of God Strengthen Me?
© 2019 by David B. McWilliams

Reformation Heritage Books
2965 Leonard St. NE
Grand Rapids, MI 49525
616-977-0889
orders@heritagebooks.org
www.heritagebooks.org

Printed in the United States of America
19 20 21 22 23 24/10 9 8 7 6 5 4 3 2 1

ISBN 978-1-60178-696-8
ISBN 978-1-60178-697-5 (e-pub)

For additional Reformed literature, request a free book list from Reformation Heritage Books at the above regular or e-mail address.

HOW SHOULD THE
SOVEREIGNTY OF GOD
STRENGTHEN ME?

———————❧———————

The LORD hath prepared his throne in the heavens; and his kingdom ruleth over all.
—Psalm 103:19

There is nothing more comforting and encouraging to a child of God than the Scripture's teaching on God's sovereignty. It is a truth for which Christians should earnestly contend, a rock on which we must depend, a comfort that steadies our ship in the gale, a magnet that attracts our prayers, and the immovable reality that strengthens our resolve. Humility and repentance characterize our hearts as we know this personal, sovereign God in the midst of hardship. To Him we would attentively listen with all the hearing of the soul. "Speak, LORD; for thy servant heareth" (1 Sam. 3:9) is the heart attitude resulting from dependence on the sovereign God in our pilgrimage to our heavenly home.

To the unbelieving world, the sovereignty of God is a massive rock of offense. This is not surprising because it is on this rock that the ship of human autonomy is dashed. By contrast, the new birth gives the believer a new sense of things, a new taste and a new capacity for experiential knowledge of God. As Stephen Charnock wrote, "A man may be theologically knowing, and spiritually ignorant."[1] In the new birth, however, sinners are renewed to experiential knowledge of the truth. Those born again now depend on God's promises, long for God's presence, and believe the Lord for strength in spiritual battle. More and more God's people become "theologically knowing," but they must also grow in the ability to spiritually apply that knowledge to life. That the triune God is a decreeing God who predestines and rules providentially is the biblical truth that experientially comforts God's people in ways that the world can never comprehend. The believer knows, even when facing the incomprehensible, that nothing outside of God determines His purpose or alters His plan. God is self-contained and self-determining, and we can only know ourselves correctly when we accept God's interpretation of the universe He has made. God's sovereign rule is over all (Ps. 103:19). This comfort is founded on God's promise to keep the covenant of grace made with His own people (vv. 17–19).

How, then, does God's sovereignty strengthen us? Weak, needy, and helpless in ourselves, we are

---

1. Stephen Charnock, *The Works of Stephen Charnock* (Edinburgh: Banner of Truth, 2010), 4:69.

unable to determine our own circumstances, much less those of the world around us. How does God's sovereignty help us to confess, in the words of the old hymn, "When all around my soul gives way, He then is all my hope and stay"? What follows are four wonderful ways that God's sovereignty grips the heart and steadies the soul in hard times.

WHEN WORLD AFFAIRS SEEM OUT OF CONTROL

Soon after the Parkland, Florida, school shooting in February 2018, two young people in my congregation, fighting back tears, spoke with me. They told me about how fearful their classmates were as a result of that terrible event. They asked that I pray for them and their classmates, which I have continued to do. The youth in my congregation, and all of us, are called to trust in the God who is sovereign. The sovereignty of God gives us no minute explanation of why the Lord permits wicked sinners to break the bounds of human restraint and commit such atrocities. But the sovereignty of God strengthens His people in the knowledge that there is nothing outside of God's purview and plan, even though this is inscrutable to us.

Similarly, a gentleman attending our worship services asked my counsel in light of the "news" he watches daily and the direction of our country and world affairs. As the brother filled his mind constantly with television images and worldly commentary, his thoughts and emotions were driving him to distraction. I counseled this man toward a wiser approach to media, to much more time in God's Word and prayer, but also to constant awareness of the One who is on the throne. The psalmist reminds us, "God is the judge: he putteth down one, and setteth up another" (Ps. 75:7). Does not the Bible teach us that even the wrath of man shall praise Him (Ps. 76:10)? The words of Nebuchadnezzar after his fall and restoration encourage us: "And all the inhabitants of the earth are reputed as nothing: and he doeth according to his will in the army of heaven, and among the inhabitants of the earth: and none can stay his hand, or say unto him, What doest thou?" (Dan. 4:35).

There is a remarkable story Iain H. Murray tells in his biography of the late D. Martyn Lloyd-Jones, who ministered long and fruitfully at Westminster Chapel, London. On June 18, 1944, during the Sunday morning service, a German bomber was heard approaching while Lloyd-Jones was praying the pastoral prayer. Despite the great noise, he continued to pray until he could no longer hear himself. Then the engine cut out, and after a period of silence, the bomb exploded only a few yards from the chapel, cracking its structure and sending dust and plaster all over those under its roof. Nearby, it was later discovered, over sixty people were killed and three hundred injured. The congregation rose collectively to its feet at the impact of the bomb, but after a brief pause, Lloyd-Jones completed his prayer. Mr. Marsh, church secretary, ascended to the pulpit, dusting off both it and the minster. The service continued, but it was said that the congregation had been steadied by the pastor's prayer and he had prayed "as one who believed that a Christian has a right to be at peace in any situation."[2] Why is a Christian able to be at peace in any situation? It is because of the sovereignty of God.

I am far from suggesting that this sense of calm will always reign in the believer's heart. But we as believers have the God-given right for peace in any situation because of the character of the One in whom we trust: "What time I am afraid, I will trust in thee. In God I will praise his word, in God I have put my trust; I will not fear what flesh can do unto me" (Ps. 56:3–4). Whether the bomb falls on us or around us, our God does not change, and His plan for us is perfect; therefore, we can be strengthened and steadied by that knowledge no matter what we may read or hear on the news. Various networks and agencies reporting what they call the news have no way of knowing the real news, the news behind the news—namely, that our God rules and reigns and is bringing His plan to perfect fruition despite the sin of man and even through it.

---

2. Iain H. Murray, *D. Martyn Lloyd-Jones: The Fight of Faith* (Edinburgh: Banner of Truth, 1990), 2:114–15.

2) WHEN WE ARE TEMPTED TO DESPAIR FOR THE SUCCESS OF THE GOSPEL

Believers may be tempted to worry not only about world events and the moral collapse of culture but also about the success of the gospel in the world. Sometimes I hear these fears expressed in the prayers of the saints in corporate prayer meetings: "Lord, where is the success of the gospel? So few believe in Christ; so much blatant humanism and self-salvation pervade the professing church; so many heresies accost us; and there is so much unfaithfulness in doctrine, worship, and life." These prayers show that the true child of God can feel overwhelmed and discouraged. While it is good that we take these feelings to the Father in prayer, we also need to submit our hearts to the teaching of God's Word. How do we keep our balance in the whirl of doctrinal error, man-centered preaching, and pervasive carelessness about truth? Where do we turn for help and sustenance? We turn to the reality of God's sovereignty.

In particular, Christians need to learn how to rest on the solid rock of sovereign divine election. Just as election is a necessary plank in our personal assurance of faith and steadies our walk and puts steel in our backbones, it also gives confidence in God's redemptive plan for others. This biblical doctrine has not been revealed to perturb us but rather to assure us and to give us confidence on our pilgrimage to the Celestial City. In this too, "we walk by faith, not by sight" (2 Cor. 5:7).

What is election, and how does this help us to overcome a doubting and depressing approach to the extension of the gospel in the world? Election is God's sovereign, loving determination to save those whom He has chosen in Christ before creation, not because of anything in them but for His own glory (Acts 13:48; Rom. 9:6–13; Eph. 1:4, 11; 2 Thess. 2:13; 2 Tim. 1:9). It is as if the decree of God is His great bow, and the arrow placed in it is His saving love and mercy. The decree lets love fly, and come what may, no matter the obstacles, it must hit its target. There may be obstacles, such as opposition to the preaching of the gospel, government persecution of ministers of the Word, or sin in the heart of the object of His love. No matter. This great arrow of love and mercy will fly over, around, and even through opposition into the heart of the chosen target. Imagine a prayer meeting in which this great theme is extolled. Do you think we would leave with encouraged hearts?

When we are tempted to worry about the church, the few that are saved, and the denial of Christ right and left, the remedy is to look to Christ, in whom are His elect people, to allow the knowledge of the sovereignty of God to take charge of our thinking and to lift up our heads in praise. Election is the supreme expression of God's love to us, and such love will not fail in its purpose for you or in God's plan for His people. Indeed, the plan of God is an eternal plan, and this puts great strength in the rope that holds our hearts steady in the fray.

Elijah cried to the Lord in fatigue and with just such concern in 1 Kings 19, summarized for the encouragement of God's people by Paul in Romans 11:1–7. Elijah complained to the Lord as if he were alone and the work of gospel conquest was floundering: "Lord, they have killed thy prophets, and digged down thine altars; and I am left alone, and they seek my life" (Rom. 11:3). How did God answer? "I have reserved to myself seven thousand men, who have not bowed the knee to the image of Baal" (v. 4). This is the encouragement of electing grace.

> Even so then at this present time also there is a remnant according to the election of grace. And if by grace, then is it no more of works: otherwise grace is no more grace. But if it be of works, then is it no more grace: otherwise work is no more work. What then? Israel hath not obtained that which he seeketh for; but the election hath obtained it, and the rest were blinded. (vv. 5–7)

Paul's purpose in Romans 11 was to encourage his readers that there was a place in God's ongoing plan for the Jewish people, but the principle is more broadly applicable: God's electing grace will accomplish its purpose, and God's saved people must remember that things are not what they seem. God is working out His saving purpose even in the midst of darkness; nothing and no one can stop God's sovereign purpose from its fruition.

How does the sovereignty of God encourage us when the news headlines disturb our peace, when the church often seems lethargic, when our souls burn to see lost sinners know the Lord, or when the "truth is fallen in the street" (Isa. 59:14)? Look up and take heart; God rules and reigns. He is sovereign over all things for His own glory. The false religion of free will shall not triumph, but the true religion of free grace will succeed and triumph. The gospel will be preached; the Lord will direct the arrow sent out from the bow of His eternal decree to its appointed target. God's sovereign purpose will succeed, it must succeed, and it cannot fail because God is God. "Not unto us, O LORD, not unto us, but unto thy name give glory, for thy mercy, and for thy truth's sake" (Ps. 115:1). The wicked cannot thwart God's plan: "The LORD hath made all things for himself: yea, even the wicked for the day of evil" (Prov. 16:4). The Lord's plan in the eternal covenant shall be accomplished: "My covenant will I not break, nor alter the thing that is gone out of my lips" (Ps. 89:34). Do not allow the news to bring you to despair about gospel success, for "our God is in the heavens: he hath done whatsoever he hath pleased" (Ps. 115:3).

A very moving example of trusting God to bless His gospel in the world is found in the biography of John Calvin and the spread of the Reformed faith in France. Five young ministerial students from Geneva and Lausanne were captured by Roman Catholic authorities in Lyon. Calvin did all within his power to secure their release, but to no avail. Calvin wrote to encourage them as they awaited execution:

> Meanwhile be the Son of God glorified by our shame. Let us be consoled with the sure testimony that we are persecuted and mocked for no other reason than that we believe in the living God. This is sufficient cause to despise the whole world with its pride, till we be gathered into that Everlasting Kingdom where we shall fully enjoy those blessings which we now only possess in hope.[3]

We learn that the five so steadfastly confessed their faith that their example, rather than encouraging backsliding, had the opposite effect. The congregation was strengthened in every way. Even a highway robber in prison was converted under their influence. When they were led to the stake for execution, the young martyrs sang Psalm 9 and recited the Apostles' Creed, particularly being careful that all Roman Catholics heard "conceived by the Holy Ghost: born of the virgin Mary." As the fire leapt and engulfed them, they strengthened each other, crying out, "Courage, brother, courage!" "Thus died Calvinists."[4] Thus died these five young men who believed in the sovereignty of God, electing grace, and the certain fulfillment of God's purpose for His church.

---

3. Emanuel Stickelberger, *Calvin* (Exeter, England: James Clarke, 1959), 117.

4. Stickelberger, *Calvin*, 118.

God is still God. Are you discouraged about the few who believe, the persecution of Christ's church in the world, the apparent weakness of our witness despite strenuous effort to spread the gospel far and wide? Think again. God is working out His purpose, and He will, even through imprisoned youths and their deaths, succeed in His plan to reach and save His people from sin.

In a lecture, Cornelius Van Til pointed out that on D–Day General Eisenhower had in his pocket a note that said, in effect, if the invasion failed he alone was to be held responsible. Van Til was quick to say that Christ has no such paper in His pocket! Does your heart not say "amen" to that reality? God's elect infallibly will be saved; God will glorify His Son; and God's purpose, plan, and end for the world will be brought to fruition. The Holy Spirit will call and regenerate chosen sinners (John 3:6–7; 6:44–45, 65) and completely apply the purchased redemption. The elect will be kept to the end and raised in the last day (John 6:37–40; Phil. 1:6), and God's redemptive plan will be fulfilled to the praise of His Son's glory (Eph. 1:12).

WHEN WE ARE CALLED TO ENDURE HARDSHIP

Do you believe that God is sovereign in your trials? The outworking of God's eternal plan is called *providence*. We have been speaking of this truth all along, but now it is time to unpack its meaning more fully, especially in relation to our trials. The Westminster

Shorter Catechism summarizes the biblical teaching
on providence with this wonderfully precise defini-
tion in the answer to question 11, "What are God's
works of providence?" The catechism answers, "God's
works of providence are His most holy, wise and powerful preserving and governing all His creatures, and
all their actions." This truth of God's providence is
indispensible for faithful Christian living and is especially filled with comfort and strength in the midst
of trials. Indeed, John Calvin rightly said that "igno-
rance of providence is the ultimate of all miseries; the
highest blessedness lies in the knowledge of it."[5] Pointing to the pastoral use of providence, Calvin insisted
that living out of this truth will bring "immeasurable
felicity" to a godly mind.[6] "Gratitude of mind for the
favorable outcome of things, patience in adversity,
and also incredible freedom from worry about the
future all necessarily follow upon this knowledge."[7]

Christian, are you gripped by the reality that we
do not live in a world of chance? "Are not five sparrows sold for two farthings, and not one of them is
forgotten before God?" said our Lord. "But even the
very hairs of your head are all numbered. Fear not
therefore: ye are of more value than many sparrows"
(Luke 12:6–7). The encouragement of providence in

---

5. John Calvin, *The Institutes of the Christian Religion* (Philadelphia:
Westminster Press, 1960), 1.17.11.

6. Calvin, *Institutes*, 1.17.9.

7. Calvin, *Institutes*, 1.17.7.

this passage is (1) that because God is infinite, even the smallest creatures are in God's sovereign control; (2) you are of more value than many sparrows, so God will not forget you; (3) even the mundane (the hair on our head) is under God's providential care, so how much more your sighs, groans, and suffering; (4) therefore, in all things walk faithfully and confess Christ. We do not live in a chance universe, but in a universe in which God is intimately, lovingly, wisely, albeit mysteriously guiding the lives of His children.

This truth, expressed by Jesus in Luke 12 and throughout Scripture, presupposes God's decree. God has an overarching plan. It is amazing that people will have plans and yet balk at the thought that God has a purposeful plan for His own people. If we were planning to build a house, we would engage an architect who would draw plans and have an end in view. How much more does the sovereign God have a plan and purpose for His people and for His world? Nothing can thwart the plan of the infinite, eternal, and unchangeable God. Our architect's drawing may change along the way. He may find it necessary to change plans to suit his client's desires. This is not true of the plan of the triune God. God's eternal, volitional, independent, absolute plan will not alter. His plan infallibly includes the salvation of His people. It includes the predestined cross (Acts 2:23) and the calling of those whom He has loved with an eternal love. This plan includes the preservation and ultimate glorification of the saints.

The importance of getting these truths way down deep into our hearts can hardly be overstressed. God's eternal, comprehensive decree is not revealed to confuse us but to exalt God in our hearts and to comfort us in our pilgrimage to the Celestial City. Stimulate your love for this truth! Find sweet rest here. Things are hard, but God says all will be well (Rom. 8:28). Holding firmly to this reality is essential to biblical piety. In heavy and hard providences we can know that those things are not chance, random events but providences ordained of the Lord for His glory and for our good. With Joseph, as he surveyed the circuitous ways of God's providence, we can confess: "But as for you, ye thought evil against me; but God meant it unto good" (Gen. 50:20). In the vast configuration of things, His all-encompassing plan, God has not forgotten you, His child. The Lord is in the details—the common and not so common. Give your heart to God in this. The soul of piety is learning to delight in God while in the heat of trials and to contemplate worshipfully God's attributes for our sustenance. John Owen said arrestingly:

> The more sublime and glorious—the more inaccessible unto sense and reason—the things are which we believe; the more we change into the image of God, in the exercise of faith upon them.... Faith which is truly divine, is never more in its proper exercise—doth never more elevate the soul into conformity unto God—than when it acts in the contemplation

and admiration of the most incomprehensible mysteries which are proposed unto it by divine revelation.[8]

Even though Owen is particularly referencing the Trinity and the incarnation of our Lord in this passage, his observation is applicable equally to our theme, God's sovereign decree and providence. Learning to meditate on this theme, turning it over in our mind, and taking it into our very soul—this is the way to becoming like Christ, who trusted in God even in the agony of the cross (Ps. 22:1–18).

Often our lives are lived in the valley of weeping. The Lord is with His people, however, and it is essential to live from the promises of God traceable to His good and wise decree. The *manner* of God's decree is unknown to us (Rom. 11:33–36), but the *reality* of God's decree sustains us. All things are moving toward their appointed end for the good of God's people (Rom. 8:28). Just as two rails seem to meet at a distance, so the ultimate purpose of God is one. God holds in his hands men's thoughts and ways. As Proverbs 21:1 reminds us, "The king's heart is in the hand of the LORD, as the rivers of water: he turneth it withersoever he will."

The Bible teems with examples, but note this one. The Lord had promised that the Messiah would be

---

8. John Owen, *The Works of John Owen* (Edinburgh: Banner of Truth, 1972), 1:50.

born in Bethlehem (Mic. 5:2). Mary must give birth to the child whom she carries by virtue of the virginal conception through the Holy Spirit's miraculous power. How will they be moved to go to Bethlehem? The Lord sovereignly worked in the heart of Caesar Augustus to take a census requiring that everyone return for a time to their place of birth. There the Christ is born (Luke 2:1–7). Augustus had a plan to take a Roman census, but the plan behind the plan was God's. "It was Caesar's whim; but it was God's decree."[9] God always fulfills His decree (Eph. 1:11). In Isaiah 46:10 God says, "My counsel shall stand, and I will do all my pleasure." Believer, do you not love this truth? Do you feel strength enter your soul as we together contemplate it?

Sparrows are not sold nor do they fall without God. There are no contingencies from God's perspective. Your God deserves to be treated with complete confidence—no matter what trials you face. He is in complete control. Allow sacred Scripture to steady your soul: "The counsel of the LORD standeth for ever, the thoughts of his heart to all generations" (Ps. 33:11). God's plan does not change because He does not change (Num. 23:19; 1 Sam. 15:29; Mal. 3:6; James 1:17).

This is not fatalism, impersonal, capricious, and haphazard. Our souls come to delight in and are

---

9. C. H. Spurgeon, *The New Park Street Pulpit* (Pasadena Tex.: Pilgrim Publications, 1975), 2:28.

strengthened by the plan of the triune, infinitely personal God, wise and holy. Whatever your joys, whatever your trials, whatever your sorrows, the Lord reigns. I once heard the story of a minister who hurried to visit a family in the church because a child had suddenly died. What would he say to this grieving family? How would he comfort them? As I remember, this is what he said: "I don't know why this has happened, and, to be honest, I don't think God does either." He went on to tell the family that God can bring good out of tragedy. Small comfort! To tell our Christian families that we live in a chance universe, that God is taken by surprise, and that the death of a child had nothing to do with God's sovereign plan is to remove all comfort and to fill the heart with fear. But to tell our grieving Christian families, while never minimizing their pain, that there is purpose and meaning in even the greatest tragedies; that we do not live in a chance universe; and that, moreover, even though such things are inscrutable to us they are not to our loving Lord is to set the thoughts of God's people on the right trajectory, bringing glory to God in the midst of suffering. This will help Christians to grieve with hope.

The great paradigm for this, to which we must return time and again, is the cross. The cross was no accident. It was planned by God for our salvation before the foundations of the world were laid. Peter preached this truth on the day of Pentecost: "Him, being delivered by the determinate counsel and foreknowledge of God, ye have taken, and by wicked hands have crucified and slain" (Acts 2:23). Here Peter proclaims that wicked men were completely responsible for their sinful deed of crucifying our Lord, but the cross was no accident. God planned it in sovereign decree.

Similarly, in Acts 4, Peter and John were imprisoned. What did the church do? The church prayed with a deep sense of reliance on the sovereign God: "Lord, thou art God, which hast made heaven, and earth, and the sea, and all that in them is" (v. 24). These praying Christians next acknowledged that the opposition they faced was prophesied long ago, and they found strength in the pronouncements of the sovereign God in Psalm 2: "Who by the mouth of thy servant David hast said, Why did the heathen rage, and the people imagine vain things? The kings of the earth stood up, and the rulers were gathered together against the Lord, and against his Christ" (vv. 25–26). Next, in view of the expectation of violent opposition against Christ in Psalm 2, these praying believers pointed to the sinful rebellion of those who put to death our Lord: "For of a truth against thy holy child Jesus, whom thou hast anointed, both Herod, and Pontius Pilate, with the Gentiles, and the people of Israel, were gathered together" (v. 27). What comfort did the believers take from this truth, anchoring their thoughts in God's sovereignty and the promises of Psalm 2? They were comforted and strengthened by the same theme and perspective that we found in Acts 2:23. Herod, Pilate, Gentiles, and Israelites "were gathered together, for to do whatsoever thy hand and thy counsel determined before to be done" (Acts 4:27–28). The predetermined crucifixion of Jesus was the paradigm for the church's prayer and viewpoint. Note what the church did and learn from their perspective. First, note that in trouble they prayed. They did not draw the false conclusion that because God had foreordained the persecution they now faced, prayer was unnecessary. Predestination does not lead to fatalistic inactivity. But they also did not wring their hands and pray unworthily of God, as if He were incapable of intervening and may have been surprised by the persecution of the church. No, rather, predestination and providence made them mighty in prayer, and their perspective on the entire event held together the twin truths that the persecuting sinners were fully responsible for what they did and that God sovereignly decreed their circumstances. There would have been no comfort had they falsely thought, "We do not know why this has happened, and God does not either." Perish such false thinking forever! The God to whom the church prayed is the God who in Psalm 2 predicts opposition to Christ but who also will laugh the ungodly to scorn and will dash them in pieces like a potter's vessel.

Whatever joys, sorrows, and circumstances, believers have the rock-ribbed assurance that these things are ordained of the Lord for His glory and for their good. You are not called to explain it, but

you are called to believe it and to adore God in the
process. Note that just one chapter before Luke 12,
in which our Lord Jesus gives the comfort that sparrows and the hair on our heads illustrate the minute
care of God, the Lord Jesus taught His disciples to
pray, saying, "Our Father which art in heaven" (11:2).
It may not always be apparent that God is showing
fatherly care of us in the hardest of times and circumstances, but He is.

My wife and I remember worshiping in a reverent,
Presbyterian service many years ago on a morning
when the minister was baptizing a child. When he
took the little fair-skinned baby from his father and
held him against his black pulpit gown, the baby
immediately began to cry—as if he had been pinched!
I think that we have never since heard a baby cry and
scream as much as during that baptism. After baptizing the child, the minister placed the infant back into
his father's arms. Immediately, all was still and silent.
When the pastor walked behind the pulpit, he looked
gravely over the congregation and said, "Would that
we were all so secure in our heavenly Father's arms."
He meant, of course, that every Christian is secure
but that we do not always perceive the security that
belongs to us as believers. When trouble comes and
"we walk by faith, not by sight" (2 Cor. 5:7), what
must be the language of the child of God? We must
recognize that there is more here than meets the eye
and therefore confess, "Though he slay me, yet will I
trust in him" (Job 13:15).

When going through trouble I urge you to keep these five truths in mind: (1) in this trial the Father is glorifying His Son; (2) God is working even when you cannot see it (2 Kings 6:17–20); (3) this hard thing is calling you to stand in awe of God's character and attributes (Job 42:5); (4) the cross demonstrates God's predestinating decree and is the demonstration of His love (Acts 2:23; Rom. 5:8). Never doubt God's love, believer. Many times you may say, "I do not understand" while simultaneously confessing, "I know what is true and that His loving purpose for me is being worked out (Rom. 8:28). Whatever my God is doing, the cross is the paradigm. I can never doubt His love." This is God's antidote to self-pity and road to spiritual triumph. (5) Finally, in addition, you must keep in mind always that you are in union with Christ and that through the troubles you endure, God, in His sovereignty, is conforming you to the image of His Son. Through union with Christ, as Louis Berkhof beautifully observed,

> Believers are changed into the image of Christ *according to his human nature.* What Christ effects in His people is in a sense a replica or reproduction of what took place with Him. Not only objectively, but also in a subjective sense they suffer, bear the cross, are crucified, die, and are raised in newness of life, with Christ. They share in a measure the experiences of their Lord,

Matt. 16:24; Rom. 6:5; Gal. 2:20; Col. 1:24; 2:12; 3:1;
1 Peter 4:13.[10]

God is always good to His people. If we are
burned at the stake, God is good to His people.
How often when things are going well do we say,
"God is good." Yes, but do we say "God is good"
when things seem to go badly? That is the difference
between theoretical knowledge of God and a deep,
trusting, growing biblical piety that fills the heart
and controls our lives. When things do not turn out
pleasantly, do you know, experientially, that God
is in this also, that your heavenly Father is for you
in this and that special love is being shown to you
despite appearances?

Applying the knowledge of God's sovereignty
will help us in trials in four ways. First, the sovereignty of God, experientially known and loved,
produces a confident and trusting heart. Knowing in
the heat of battle that the Father chose us, the Son
died for us, and the Spirit calls us but also that an
indispensable part of God's plan is that providence
directs us will produce deep, confident, dependent
trust. What appear to be "accidents" in life are the
inexplicable paths by which the Lord is steering His
people where He wants them to be. In these ways He
keeps our tent stakes loose and gives us a longing

10. Louis Berkhof, *Systematic Theology* (Grand Rapids: Eerdmans, 1972), 451.

for our heavenly home. The sovereignty of God produces trust that amazes others and witnesses to God's greatness. In an article "Is the Shorter Catechism Worthwhile?," B. B. Warfield tells of an Army officer in a western city in a time of violent rioting. There was danger everywhere, but the officer saw another man with great calm "whose very demeanor inspired confidence." Turning to this man the officer asked: "What is the chief end of man?" The stalwart gentleman immediately answered: "Man's chief end is to glorify God and to enjoy him forever." The officer said, "I knew you were a Shorter Catechism boy," and the other said, "That was just what I was thinking of you." Warfield adds: "It is worthwhile to be a Shorter Catechism boy. They grow to be men. And better than that, they are exceedingly apt to grow to be men of God."[11] So the sovereignty of God gives us confidence.

Second, the sovereignty of God gives God's people a peaceful heart in trials. The trouble we experience is not accidental from God's perspective, and even though life in this fallen world brings grief, the believer can grieve with peace and in hope. Jonathan Edwards dwelt, it would seem, moment by moment on the sovereignty and attributes of God and was possessed of a majestic calm. When he was unjustly dismissed as minister from his beloved congregation,

---

11. B. B. Warfield, *Selected Shorter Writings of Benjamin B. Warfield* (Nutley, N.J.: Presbyterian and Reformed, 1970), 1:384.

an observer said that "he appeared like a man of
God, whose happiness was out of the reach of his
enemies and whose treasure was not only a future
but a present good."[12] His life demonstrated what he
had taught his flock, that the true Christian is "the
tallest and strongest saint, but the least and tenderest
child among them."[13]

Third, the knowledge of God's sovereignty in
our trials produces a praying heart. As we come to
understand that means and ends in our trials are
ordained of the Lord, so we realize that in prayer we
seek the Lord to do what He has ordained for us from
eternity. In prayer we ask for God's will to be done
and His name to be glorified. We should especially
turn to the Psalms, called by Calvin "an anatomy
of all parts of the soul," and using the words of the
psalmist learn to take our heart's needs to the God
who cares and hears the cries of His people.

Fourth, trusting in God's sovereignty in times
of pain and loss is one of God's ways of producing
in His children contented hearts. When we confess
in the language of Lord's Day 10 of the Heidelberg
Catechism that "all things come, not by chance, but
by His fatherly hand," we become "patient in adversity, thankful in prosperity," and grow in "firm trust
in our faithful God and Father, that nothing shall

12. Iain H. Murray, *Jonathan Edwards: A New Biography* (Edinburgh:
Banner of Truth, 1987), 327.

13. Murray, *Jonathan Edwards*, 329.

separate us from His love; since all creatures are so in His hand, that without His will they cannot so much as move." With contentment and confidence we can sing in advance of the day: "Great and marvellous are thy works, Lord God Almighty; just and true are thy ways, thou King of saints. Who shall not fear thee, O Lord, and glorify thy name?" (Rev. 15:3–4).

God in His sovereignty is making us holy through our trials. In those trials, take great comfort. "Now what greater comfort is there than this," asks Charnock, "that there is one who presides in the world who is so wise he cannot be mistaken, so faithful he cannot deceive, so pitiful he cannot neglect his people, and so powerful that he can make the stones even to be turned into bread if he please?"[14]

Jonathan Edwards gives us a profound image of God's providential care, even through what appear to us to be circuitous routes. He writes these words worthy of much meditation:

> God's providence may not unfitly be compared to a large and long river, having innumerable branches beginning in different regions and at a great distance one from another, and all conspiring to one common issue. After their very diverse and contrary courses which they hold for a while, yet all gathering more and more together the nearer they come to their common end, and all at length discharging themselves at

---

14. Charnock, *Works*, 1:53.

one mouth into the same ocean. The different streams of this river are ready to look like mere jumble and confusion to us because of the limitedness of our sight, whereby we can't see from one branch to another and can't see the whole at once, so as to see how all are united in one. A man who sees but one or two streams at a time can't tell what their course tends to. Their course seems very crooked, and the different streams seem to run for a while different and contrary ways. And if we view things at a distance, there seem to be innumerable obstacles and impediments in the way to hinder their ever uniting and coming to the ocean, as rocks and mountains and the like. But if we trace them they all unite at last and all come to the same issue, disgorging themselves in one into the same great ocean. Not one of all the streams fails of coming hither at last.[15]

WHEN WE ARE TEMPTED TO MAKE OUR EXPERIENCE THE STANDARD FOR INTERPRETING SUFFERING

Here we come to rock bottom: in our suffering, will we resort to autonomous resources, or to the loving, wise, though incomprehensible plan of God, regardless of what we see and may even feel for a time? Let us take the hardest of examples, the death of a child. Here we must tread with reverence and great

---

15. Jonathan Edwards, *The Works of Jonathan Edwards* (New Haven, Conn.: Yale University Press, 1989), 9:520.

empathy but, preeminently, with a desire to know and apply God's truth.

Many Christians are taught to say in the midst of such a dark moment, "God has nothing to do with this. How could He? He is loving and not the author of evil. God permitted this horrific thing. But God is not, after all, in the details. I cannot love a God who would purpose the death of a beloved child."

Every pastor knows that such thinking abounds and is not theoretical. The Christian who has been studying God's Word, however, who often has bent the knee in hard things, who has rendered worship to the Lord in the midst of trials, and who understands the Bible's doctrine of providence will not conclude when a child dies or some other tragedy strikes that we live in a chance universe. Do you remember the cross—no accident, but planned by God, who also holds men accountable for their wicked murder of the Son of God? There is a better way than that of a person who denies God's purpose in hardship.

First, this person is correct that God is not the author of evil—that is, of sin. Sin is the result of the fall of man. God hates sin. But sin has an inscrutable place in God's plan for His world. At this point we can do one of two things. We can say, "That does not make sense; therefore, I will limit God's sovereignty and believe in chance." Or we can say, "It does not make sense to me, but I know this terrible thing does have meaning, and I will not begin with my autonomy. Rather, I will submit my heart to the

God who knows best, whose plan is perfect, and I will start and continue my thinking with what He has revealed rather than with what I can perceive."

· Second, the person who denies God's purpose in hardship makes things no easier by pointing to bare permission and not to permission that is determined by sovereign purpose and plan. Why has he not solved the matter? It is because the same God who permitted could have stopped the tragedy.

Third, by adopting autonomous thinking, this person has left no room for incomprehensibility. The triune God who is infinite, eternal, and unchangeable is incomprehensible, and so must be His plan. Remember that after the Lord showed Job His great power and intimate care of His world, Job repented in dust and ashes (Job 42:6). Job rightly had confessed at the beginning of the book, "The LORD gave, and the LORD hath taken away; blessed be the name of the LORD" (1:21). It took the entire book, however, for Job to feel the awe of God's sovereignty overwhelmingly and experientially. God never explained His plan to Job. In effect, God says, "Look to Me and trust Me. You do not understand, but I do; let that suffice."

Christian, when you are tempted to fall back on your own resources in trials, resist the temptation, crucify self-sufficiency, and walk by faith rather than by sight. Do not rise up in pride or replace biblical truth with unbelief. Rather, look to God's sovereignty, especially as shown in the cross. Again and again let this be your paradigm. Say to yourself, "Was the cross an accident? No, the cross was God's perfect and necessary plan for our redemption. Did God ordain the cross? Yes, the cross is indispensable to God's plan of salvation. Did God not hate the sin that nailed His Son to the tree? Absolutely, God hates sin. Can I understand how these truths relate? No, certainly not exhaustively; it is beyond me. But, I believe God's word and in this is my comfort, hope, and strength. There is purpose in this, though I cannot see it. There is purpose in it because God is God, and therefore I do not live in a chance universe. 'Though he slay me, yet will I trust in him'" (Job 13:15).

Even in the hardest trials, we can learn to be God-centered and submissive and to have pious hearts that long for God's glory, even when suffering hurts deeply. For even these things fit into God's redemptive plan for us. We can learn to lie in the dust that God may be exalted. The growing Christian desires that God be all and in all. As Edwards put it:

> However great and glorious the creature apprehends God to be, yet if he be not sensible of the difference between God and him, so as to see that God's glory is great compared with his own, he will not be disposed to give God the glory due His name.... So much the more men exalt themselves, so much the less will they surely be disposed to exalt God.... 'Tis God's declared design that others should not "glory in his presence," which implies that 'tis his design to advance his own comparative glory.... 'Tis

the delight of a believing soul to abase itself and exalt God alone.[16]

Indeed, as he says in the same sermon, "God Glorified in Man's Dependence," "all unites in him [God] as center."[17]

Is this not what Paul confesses when contemplating the sovereignty of God in the salvation of the sinner? Should not Paul's passionate cry be our own when society falls apart, when the church struggles, and when we endure trials? Should not God's glory be our passion through it all? Should we not with Paul confess the wonder of the sovereign, incomprehensible plan of God?

> O the depth of the riches both of the wisdom and knowledge of God! how unsearchable are his judgments, and his ways past finding out! For who hath known the mind of the Lord? or who hath been his counsellor? Or who hath first given to him, and it shall be recompensed unto him again? For of him, and through him, and to him, are all things: to whom be glory for ever. Amen. (Rom. 11:33–36)

---

16. Edwards, *Works*, 17:211, 214.

17. Edwards, *Works*, 17:212.